BALANCED

Expanded Edition

CHRISTIANITY

JOHN STOTT

IVP Books

An imprint of InterVarsity Press
Downers Grove, Illinois

InterVarsity Press
P.O. Box 1400, Downers Grove, IL 60515-1426
Internet: www.ivpress.com
Email: email@ivpress.com

InterVarsity Press® is the book-publishing division of InterVarsity Christian Fellowship/
USA®, a movement of students and faculty active on campus at hundreds of universities,
colleges and schools of nursing in the United States of America, and a member movement of
the International Fellowship of Evangelical Students. For information about local and
regional activities, write Public Relations Dept., InterVarsity Christian Fellowship/USA,
6400 Schroeder Rd., P.O. Box 7895, Madison, WI 53707-7895, or visit the IVCF website
at www.intervarsity.org.

All Scripture quotations, unless otherwise indicated, are taken from THE HOLY BIBLE,
NEW INTERNATIONAL VERSION®, NIV® Copyright © 1973, 1978, 1984, 2011 by
Biblica, Inc.™ Used by permission. All rights reserved worldwide.

The material from the interview with John Stott is reproduced with the permission of Roy
McCloughry, Third Way and Christianity Today.

Cover design: Cindy Kiple
Image: © David et Myrtille /Trevillion Images

Interior design: Beth Hagenberg

ISBN 978-0-8308-4407-4 (print)
ISBN 978-0-8308-7191-9 (digital)

Printed in the United States of America ∞

Library of Congress Cataloging-in-Publication Data
A catalog record for this book is available from the Library of Congress.

P	17	16	15	14	13	12	11	10	9	8	7	6	5	4	3	2	1
Y	28	27	26	25	24	23	22	21	20	19	18	17	16	15	14		

Contents

1

Unity, Liberty & Charity

My concern is to draw attention to one of the great tragedies of contemporary Christendom, a tragedy which is especially apparent among those of us who are called (and indeed call ourselves) *evangelical* Christians. In a single word, this tragedy is *polarization*, but I shall need to spell out what I mean.

The background to the tragedy is our substantial agreement in historic, biblical Christianity. Our unity in the fundamentals of the Christian faith is a great and glorious thing. We believe in God the Father, infinite, personal, holy, the Creator and Sustainer of the universe. We believe in Jesus Christ, the unique God-man, in his virgin birth, incarnate life, authoritative teaching, atoning death, historical resurrection and personal return. We believe in the Holy Spirit, by whose special inspiration the Scriptures were written and by whose special grace today sinners are justified and born again, transformed into Christ's image, incorporated into the church and sent out into the world to serve. On these and other great biblical doctrines we stand firm by God's grace, and we stand together.

Nevertheless, we are not united. We separate from one another on matters of lesser importance. Some of these divisive issues are theological, others are temperamental. Theologically, for example, we may disagree on the precise relation between divine sovereignty and human responsibility, on the order and pastoral ministry of the church (whether it should be episcopal, presbyterian or independent) and on how far evangelical Christians may involve themselves in a "mixed" denomination without compromising themselves and their faith, on church-state relations, on who qualifies for baptism and on the volume of water to be used, on how to interpret prophecy, and on which spiritual gifts are available today and which are the most important. These are some of the issues on which equally devout and equally biblical Christians disagree. They belong to the category the Reformers called the *adiaphora*, matters "indifferent." And in these, although we shall wish to continue arguing our own conviction from Scripture according to the light we have so far been given, we should not try to press our position dogmatically on other Christian consciences, but give each other liberty in mutual love and respect. One cannot do better than quote the famous epigram attributed to a certain Rupert Meldenius and quoted by Richard Baxter:

> In essentials unity,
> In nonessentials liberty,
> In all things charity.

We are also divided from one another temperamentally. We sometimes forget that our God loves diversity and that he has created a rich profusion of human types, temperaments and personalities. Moreover, our temperament has more influence on our theology than we often realize or concede! Although our apprehension of biblical truth depends on the illumination of the Holy Spirit, it is inevitably colored by the kind of person we are, the age in which we live and the culture to which we belong. Some of us by disposition and upbringing are more intellectual than emotional, others more emotional than intellectual. Again, many people's natural habit of mind is conservative (they detest change and feel threatened by it), while others are by nature rebels against tradition (they detest monotony and find change very congenial). Such issues as these arise from basic temperamental differences. But we should not allow our temperament to control us. Rather, we should allow Scripture to judge our natural temperamental inclinations. Otherwise we shall lose our Christian equilibrium.

The title of this book is *Balanced Christianity*, for one of the greatest weaknesses which we Christians (especially evangelical Christians) display is our tendency to extremism or imbalance. It seems that there is almost no pastime the devil enjoys more than tipping Christians off balance. Although I claim neither close acquaintance with his person nor inside information into his strategy, I guess that this is one of his favorite hobbies. My conviction is that we should love balance as much as the devil hates it and seek to promote it as vigorously as he seeks to destroy it.

By our "imbalance" I mean that we seem to enjoy inhabiting one or other of the polar regions of truth. If we could straddle both poles simultaneously, we would exhibit a healthy biblical balance. Instead, we tend to polarize. Like Abraham and Lot we separate from one another. We push other people over to one pole while keeping the opposite pole as our preserve.

Theologically speaking, no one in British church history has warned us more clearly of this danger than Charles Simeon, Fellow of King's College and vicar of

Holy Trinity Church in Cambridge at the beginning of the nineteenth century. Consider this imaginary conversation with the apostle Paul which he included in a letter to a friend in 1825:

> The truth is not in the middle, and not in one extreme, but in both extremes. . . . Here are two . . . extremes, Calvinism and Arminianism. . . . "How do you move in reference to these, Paul? In a golden mean?"
>
> "No."
>
> "To one extreme?"
>
> "No!"
>
> "How then?"
>
> "To both extremes; today I am a strong Calvinist; tomorrow a strong Arminian."
>
> "Well, well, Paul, I see thou art beside thyself; go to Aristotle and learn the golden mean."

Simeon continues:

> But, my brother, I am unfortunate; I formerly read Aristotle, and liked him much; I have since read Paul and caught somewhat of his strange notions, oscillating (not vacillating) from pole to pole. Sometimes I am a high Calvinist, at other times a low Arminian, so that if extremes

will please you, I am your man; only remember,
it is not one extreme that we are to go to, but
both extremes.[1]

Simeon's words are wisdom for today. Whether our
polarizations are primarily theological or temperamental, we should avoid them. Let me give you four
examples of the folly of unnecessary polarization.

2

The first polarization concerns the intellectual and the emotional. Some Christians are so coldly intellectual that one questions whether they are warm-blooded mammals, let alone human beings, while others are so emotional that one wonders whether they have any gray matter at all.

Of the two extremes I feel bound to say that the greater danger is anti-intellectualism and a surrender to emotionalism. We see it in some evangelistic preaching, which consists of nothing but an appeal for decision with little or no proclamation of the gospel and little or no reasoning with people out of the Scriptures as the apostles did.

The same tendency is evident in the contemporary hunger for vivid, firsthand, emotional experiences, and in the enthronement of experience as the criterion of truth, whereas truth should always be the criterion of experience. I fear that this tendency is a semichristianized legacy of secular existentialism. What seems to have filtered down into the public consciousness of Martin Heidegger's famous distinction between "authentic" and "unauthentic" existence is that we must break away from every convention and discipline and from every lifestyle imposed by these, which threaten our own personal authenticity. We must above all choose to be ourselves, and think and do only what seems authentic to us at the moment. In the light of this principle, I have heard Christian young people arguing in these terms: "I cannot be expected to believe a doctrine just because it is in Scripture, but only if it authenticates itself to me as being true. You cannot expect me to go to church or read the Bible or pray just because these are Christian duties, for I can do these things only if I feel like it. And I cannot possibly love my neighbor (let alone my enemy) just because I am commanded to do so, but only if the Holy Spirit makes a love-relationship authentic and real."

Alongside the current insistence on existential experience goes a distrust and a despising of the mind. The flight from reason is a marked feature of contemporary secular life, not least in the United States.

Richard Hofstadter has documented it very effectively in his book *Anti-Intellectualism in American Life*. And a striking example of it may be found in Joe McGinniss's account of Richard Nixon's 1968 election campaign entitled *The Selling of the President 1968*. The campaign organizers were convinced that Nixon lost the election to Kennedy in 1960 because the latter had a far better television image. So they called in Marshall McLuhan to advise them on how to get Nixon to "project electronically," how to turn him from "a dry, humorless lawyer" into "a warm, animated human being." Politics, McLuhan assured them, is "only minimally a rational science." Elections, he insisted, are won not on issues but on images. "Get the voters to like the guy," and the campaign is virtually won.

It is, of course, a very serious situation when an educated nation is thus invited to surrender its political responsibility, to decline to debate the issues of the day or to make up its mind, and to vote instead by a gut reaction to candidates. But this kind of anti-intellectualism is much more serious in the Christian church. For Scripture tells us that our rationality is part of the divine image in which God has created us. He is a rational God who has made us rational beings and given us a rational revelation. To deny our rationality is therefore to deny our humanity, to become less than human beings. Scripture forbids us to behave like horses or mules which have "no understanding" and commands us instead in our understanding to be "adults" (Psalm 32:9; 1 Corinthians 14:20). Indeed, we are constantly told in the Bible that every aspect of the Christian life is impossible without the Christian use of our minds. (I have developed this theme of the Christian use of the mind in *Your Mind Matters*.)

Let me take one example, the exercise of faith. Many imagine that faith is entirely irrational. But Scripture never sets faith and reason over against each other as incompatible. On the contrary, faith can only arise and grow within us by the use of our minds. "Those who know your name trust in you" (Psalm 9:10); their trust springs from their knowledge of the trustworthiness of God's character. Again, "You will keep in perfect peace those whose minds are steadfast, because they trust in you" (Isaiah 26:3). Here trusting in God and staying the mind on God are synonyms, and perfect peace is the result.

In the light of this biblical emphasis on the place of the mind in the Christian life, what are we to say to the modern generation of emotional anti-intellectuals? I am afraid we have to say that they are loudly proclaiming themselves to be worldly Christians. For "worldliness" is not primarily a question (as I was brought up to believe) of smoking, drinking and dancing, or for that matter of makeup, movies and mini-skirts, but of the spirit of the age. If we imbibe uncritically the mood of the world (in this case, existentialism) without first subjecting it to a rigorous biblical evaluation, we have already become worldly Christians.

"It is a fundamental principle with us," said John Wesley to an early critic, "that to renounce reason is to renounce religion, that religion and reason go hand in hand, and that all irrational religion is false religion."[1]

I feel obliged to add, however, that if anti-intellectualism is dangerous, the opposite polarization is almost equally dangerous. A dry and lifeless hyper-intellectualism, an exclusive preoccupation with orthodoxy, is not New Testament Christianity. There can be no doubt that the early Christians had been deeply stirred by their experience of Jesus Christ. If the apostle Paul could write of "the surpassing worth of knowing Christ Jesus my Lord" (Philippians 3:8), and the apostle Peter could say that Christians "are filled with an inexpressible and glorious joy," (1 Peter 1:8) one can hardly accuse them of being gloomy or unfeeling.

The truth is that God has made us emotional as well as rational creatures. Not only are we warm-blooded mammals, but human beings, capable of deep feelings of love, anger, compassion, sorrow and awe. I write about this with personal conviction because it diverges somewhat from my education at an English private school. I have no wish to bite the hand that nurtured me, for I recognize how much I owe to the educational privileges I was given. Nevertheless, I find myself critical of that distinctive feature of the private school tradition known as "the stiff upper lip." Since the first external sign of deep inward emotion is often the trembling of the upper lip, to maintain a stiff one is to suppress one's emotions and to cultivate the virtues (masculine rather than feminine, Anglo-Saxon rather than Latin) of courage, fortitude and self-control. What was simply not done was for a boy to weep in public; weeping was reserved for girls and babies. Since those prewar days, however, I have read the New Testament many times and discovered that Jesus was not ashamed to express his emotions. On two separate occasions he actually burst into tears in public, first at the graveside of a friend and then at the sight of impenitent Jerusalem. But then Jesus was not brought up in the British school system!

If it is a serious peril to deny your intellect, it is a serious peril to deny your emotions. Yet many of us are doing so. Alvin Toffler writes of some American young people who already exhibit the symptoms of what he calls "future shock." He refers to a tiny beach village in Crete whose forty or fifty caves are occupied by "runaway American troglodytes, young men and women who, for the most part, have given up any further effort to cope with the exploding high-speed complexities of life." A reporter visited them in 1968 and brought them the news of the assassination of Robert F. Kennedy. Their response: silence. "No shock, no rage, no tears. Is this the new phenomenon? Running away from America and running away from emotion? I understand uninvolvement, disenchantment, even noncommitment. But where has all the feeling gone?"[2]

Pamela Hansford Johnson, who reported the sadistic horrors of the "Moors" murders between 1963 and 1965, writes that killers for gain or for gratification are "almost always lacking in what the psychologists call *affect*, that is, any capacity for entering into the feelings of others." She goes on, "We are in danger of creating an Affectless Society, in which nobody cares for anyone but himself, or for anything but instant self-gratification. We demand sex without love, violence for kicks. We are encouraging the blunting of sensibility."[3]

One of the causes of our affectless society is television. For television brings into our homes, in endless succession, scenes of violence, brutality and tragedy which make such a powerful assault on our emotions that we cannot stand it. So we do one of two things. Either we get up and switch it off, or we do something far worse: We continue to let the images flash across the screen while we switch off inside. We go on viewing, but somehow we remain emotionally unmoved.

Perhaps I may give an example from my own experience, not now of television, but of a performance of Handel's *Messiah* in the Royal Albert Hall. As the oratorio reached its climax with the Hallelujah Chorus, those majestic affirmations that "the Lord God omnipotent reigneth . . . King of kings and Lord of lords," and the final "Amen," I confess that I was deeply stirred. When the music ended the audience broke into a great roar of applause, which was a perfectly proper way of expressing their appreciation to conductor, choir, orchestra and soloists. But then, as the applause died away, all the people began reaching for hats and coats, laughing and talking and jostling one another as they made for the exits. Is it overly pious of me to say that I could not move? I had been transported into heaven, into eternity, into the presence of the great King himself. It was somehow not enough for me to clap for the *musicians*; I wanted to fall on my face and worship *God*. Am I odd to react with such profound religious emotion? Or am I right to ask what people are doing with their emotions that they can listen to an oratorio or attend a church service and remain apparently unmoved? I make no plea for *emotionalism*, for that is an artificial display, a spurious pretense. But *emotions*, genuine feelings legitimately aroused—these must be expressed, not suffocated.

What, then, is the true relation between the intellectual and the emotional? Muhammed Iqbal—the lawyer and poet who became president of the Muslim League, paved the way for a separate Pakistan and worked for a new spiritual understanding between East and West—wrote in one of his poems,

> In the West intellect is the source of life,
> In the East love is the basis of life.
> Through love intellect grows acquainted with
> 　　　Reality,
> And intellect gives stability to the work of love.
> Arise, and lay the foundations of a new world,
> By wedding intellect to love.

This is finely said. But intellect is not the prerogative of the West, nor love (or emotion) of the East. Some nations and races may indeed have more of the one or the other, but intellect and emotion cannot be restricted to some temperaments or some cultures. For both are part of all the humanity which

God has created. Both therefore belong to an authentic human experience.

In particular, nothing sets the heart on fire like truth. Truth is not cold and dry. On the contrary, it is warm and passionate. And whenever new vistas of God's truth open up to us, we cannot just contemplate. We are stirred to respond, whether to penitence or to anger or to love or to worship. Think of the two disciples walking to Emmaus on the first Easter afternoon while the risen Lord spoke to them. When he vanished, they said to each other, "Were not our hearts burning within us while he talked with us on the road and opened the Scriptures to us?" (Luke 24:32). They had an emotional experience all right that afternoon. They described their sensation as a burning heart. And what was the cause of their spiritual heartburn? It was Christ's opening the Scriptures to them!

It should be the same today. Whenever we read the Scripture and Christ opens it up to us so that we grasp fresh truth in it, our hearts should burn within us. As F. W. Faber once said, "Deep theology is the best fuel of devotion; it readily catches fire, and once kindled it burns long."[4]

This true combination of intellect and emotion should be apparent in the preaching as well as in the understanding of God's Word. No one has expressed this better than Martyn Lloyd-Jones, who gives this striking definition of preaching:

> What is preaching? Logic on fire! Eloquent reason! Are these contradictions? Of course they are not. Reason concerning this Truth ought to be mightily eloquent, as you see it in the case of the Apostle Paul and others. It is theology on fire. And a theology which does not take fire, I maintain, is a defective theology; or at least the man's understanding of it is defective. Preaching is theology coming through a man who is on fire.[5]

3

Conservative & Radical

The second unnecessary polarization in the contemporary church is between *conservatives* and *radicals*. We must begin by defining these terms. By conservatives we are referring to people who are determined to conserve or preserve the past and are therefore resistant to change. By radicals we are referring to people who are in rebellion against what is inherited from the past and therefore are agitating for change.

In 1968 I attended as an "adviser" the Fourth Assembly of the World Council of Churches at Uppsala in Sweden. I discovered on arrival that we were all immediately categorized, especially in the newspaper which was published daily. We were either rather scornfully dismissed as conservative, reactionary, status quo, stuck-in-the-mud traditionalists, or enthusiastically embraced as reforming, revolutionary radicals! But this is a ludicrous categorization. Every balanced Christian should have a foot in both camps.

Let me now define more precisely in what sense every Christian should be both a conservative and a radical.

Every Christian should be conservative because the whole church is called by God to conserve his revelation, to "guard the deposit," to "contend for the faith that was once for all entrusted to God's holy people" (see 1 Timothy 6:20; 2 Timothy 1:14; Jude 3). The church's task is not to keep inventing new gospels, new theologies, new moralities and new Christianities, but rather to be a faithful guardian of the one and only eternal gospel. For the self-revelation of God has reached its completion in his Son Jesus Christ and in the apostolic witness to Christ preserved in the New Testament. It cannot be altered in any way, whether by addition or by modification. It is changeless in truth and authority.

The authors of the book *Growing into Union* expressed this point with forcefulness:

> The Church's first task is to keep the good news intact. It is better to speak of the habit of mind which this calling requires as "conservationist" rather than "conservative," for the latter word

can easily suggest an antiquarian addiction to what is old for its own sake and a blanket resistance to new thinking, and this is not what we are talking about at all. Antiquarianism and obscurantism are vices of the Christian mind, but Conservationism is among its virtues.[1]

Some Christians, however, do not limit their conservatism to their biblical theology. For the fact is that they are conservative by temperament. They are therefore conservative in their politics and in their social outlook, in their lifestyle, dress-style, hairstyle, beard-style and every other kind of style you care to mention! They are not just stuck in the mud; the mud has set like concrete. Change of every kind is anathema to them. They are like the English duke who during his student days at Cambridge University remarked, "Any change at any time for any reason is to be deplored!" Their favorite slogan is, "As it was in the beginning, is now and ever shall be, world without end. Amen!"

Radicals, on the other hand, ask awkward questions of the Establishment. They regard no tradition, no convention and no institution (however ancient) as sacrosanct. They reverence no sacred cows. On the contrary, radicals are prepared to subject everything inherited from the past to critical scrutiny.

And their scrutiny often leads them to want thoroughgoing reform, even revolution (though not, if they are Christians, by violence).

Radicals recognize the rapidity with which the world scene is changing today. They do not feel particularly threatened by it nor is their first instinct to behave like King Canute and try to arrest the rising tide of change. Alvin Toffler defines "future shock," the expression he invented as a parallel to "culture shock," in these terms: "Future shock is the dizzying disorientation brought on by the premature arrival of the future. It may well be the most important disease of tomorrow."[2] But radicals are not shocked by it. Knowing that change is inevitable, they welcome it and adjust to it. They even sometimes initiate it.

It appears then, at first sight, that conservatives and radicals are in opposition to one another and that we cannot help polarizing on this issue. But this is not so.

It is not sufficiently understood that our Lord Jesus Christ was at one and the same time a conservative and a radical, although in different spheres. There is no question that he was conservative in his attitude to the Scripture. "Scripture cannot be set aside," he said. "I have not come to abolish [the Law and the Prophets] but to fulfill them." Again, "not the smallest letter, not the least stroke of a pen, will by any means disappear from the Law until everything is accomplished" (John 10:35; Matthew 5:17-18). One of Jesus' chief complaints against contemporary Jewish leaders concerned their disrespect for Old Testament Scripture and their lack of a true submission to its divine authority.

But Jesus may also be truly described as a radical. He was a keen, fearless critic of the Jewish Establishment, not only because of their insufficient loyalty to God's Word but also because of their exaggerated loyalty to their own human traditions. Jesus had the temerity to sweep away centuries of inherited tradition ("the tradition of the elders") in order that God's Word might again be seen and obeyed (Mark 7:1-13). He was also daring in his breaches of social convention. He insisted on caring for those sections of the community which were normally despised. He spoke to women in public, which in his day was not done. He invited children to come to him, although in Roman society unwanted children were commonly "exposed" or dumped, and his own disciples took it for granted that he would not want to be bothered with them. He allowed prostitutes to touch him (Pharisees recoiled from them in horror) and himself actually touched an untouchable leper (Pharisees threw stones at them to make them keep their distance). In these and other ways Jesus refused to be bound by human custom; his mind and conscience were bound by God's Word alone.

Thus Jesus was a unique combination of the conservative and the radical, conservative toward Scripture and radical in his scrutiny (his *biblical* scrutiny) of everything else.

Now the disciple is not above his teacher, as Jesus often said. So if Jesus could combine radicalism with conservatism so can we who claim to follow him. Indeed, we must if we would be loyal to him. There is an urgent need for more *RCs* to emerge in the church, standing now not for Roman Catholics but for Radical Conservatives, and a need for evangelical Christians to develop a more critical discernment between what may not be changed and what may and even must.

Let me give an example of what may not be changed. It was customary in former days for the Lord's Prayer, the Ten Commandments and the Apostles' Creed to be painted on the east wall of many English churches for everybody to see and read. In one village church the lettering had faded, and a local decorator was engaged to touch up the paint where necessary. In due course, so the story goes, the church council was startled by the ambiguity of the account submitted to them. Being before the age of decimalization, it read as follows:

To repairing the Lord's Prayer 10s
To three new Commandments 12s
To making a completely new Creed . . . 17s 6d

On the other hand, although we have no authority
to alter either the creed or the commandments
which God has revealed, yet (as Leighton Ford rightly
said at the 1969 American Congress on Evangelism in
Minneapolis) "God is not tied to seventeenth-century
English, nor to eighteenth-century hymns, nor to
nineteenth-century architecture, nor to twentieth-
century clichés," nor (one might add) to much else
besides. Although he himself never changes, nor
does his revelation, yet he is also a God on the move,
ever calling his people out to fresh and adventurous
enterprises.

More particularly, we all need to discern more
clearly between Scripture and culture. For Scripture is
the eternal, unchanging Word of God. But culture is
an amalgam of ecclesiastical tradition, social convention and artistic creativity. Whatever "authority"
culture may have is derived only from church and
community. It cannot claim an immunity to criticism
or reform. On the contrary, culture changes from age
to age and from place to place. Moreover, we Christians, who say we desire to live under the authority of

God's Word, should subject our own contemporary culture to continuous biblical scrutiny. Far from resenting or resisting cultural change, we should be in the forefront of those who propose and work for its progressive modification in order to make it more truly expressive of the dignity of humanity and more pleasing to the God who created us.

On a visit to the United States I was impressed by a group of students I met at Trinity Evangelical Divinity School in Deerfield, Illinois. They had come from a variety of different backgrounds but found themselves united in their commitment to biblical Christianity, in their disenchantment with much contemporary American Christianity and in their resolve to discover a radical application of biblical Christianity to the big issues of the day. So they coalesced into a study and prayer group out of which grew the People's Christian Coalition, whose organ was *The Post-American* (now called *Sojourners*). Its first issue in February, 1971, depicted on the front cover the Lord Jesus, thorn-crowned, handcuffed and draped with the Stars and Stripes. Some thought the picture bordered on blasphemy. But I did not share this reaction. Rather it was a genuine expression of their concern for the honor of Christ. Jim Wallis voiced this in his editorial:

The offense of established religion is the proclamation and practice of a caricature of Christianity so inculturated, domesticated and lifeless
that our generation easily and naturally rejects it.
. . . We find that the American church is in captivity to the values and lifestyle of our culture.
. . . The American captivity of the church has re-
sulted in the disastrous equation of the American
way of life with the Christian way of life.

Exactly the same could be said of the cultural expression of Christianity in other parts of the world. It
is a major problem in many churches of the Third
World, which were planted by missions from Europe
and North America and are now seeking their own
indigenous identity. They are faced with two cultural
problems. The first concerns native or tribal culture,
perhaps especially in Africa. National Christian
leaders recognize that whereas some traditional African customs reflect their pagan origins and are incompatible with Christian faith, love and righteousness, others not only are morally and spiritually
harmless but can actually be subjected to the lordship
of Christ and contribute to the enrichment of life.

The second problem concerns the alien culture
(whether European or American) which all too often

was imported into the Third World along with the gospel. It is partly because this cultural invasion has seemed to many an affront to their own national dignity that the cry has arisen to "get rid of the white man's religion." Of course the cry is mistaken. For Christianity belongs neither to the white man nor to any other group of men. Jesus Christ is Lord of every race, country and age without any discrimination. Nevertheless, it is right for Africans, Asians and Latin Americans to seek to develop their own indigenous expressions of Christian truth and life. René Padilla made an eloquent appeal for this at the International Congress on World Evangelization in Lausanne in July, 1974, when he castigated what he called "culture Christianity."

So Christian leaders of younger churches need great wisdom to discern not just between national and imported cultures but also between what in both cultures is honoring to Christ and what is dishonoring, between what is valuable and what is worthless. They also need courage to retain the one and to reject the other.

European Christianity, too, whose roots reach back nearly two thousand years, is deeply embedded in the culture of the centuries. It is not without significance that we can talk about Lutheran*ism*, Anglican*ism*,

Presbyterian*ism*, Method*ism* and even Brethren*ism*. Each is a traditional or cultural form of historic Christianity. That form colors not only our doctrinal formularies, but our liturgy (or nonliturgy) and music, our church buildings and their decor, the respective roles of clergy and laity in the church, our printing and publicity, our pastoral and evangelistic methods, in fact everything we do as churches. And *all* of it should be subjected to regular, critical, biblical investigation.

So when we resist change, whether in church or society, we need to ask whether in reality it is Scripture we are defending (as it is our custom stoutly to insist) or rather some cherished tradition of the ecclesiastical elders or of our cultural heritage. This is not to say that all traditions, simply because they are traditional, must at all costs be swept away. Uncritical iconoclasm is as stupid as uncritical conservatism, and is sometimes more dangerous. What I am emphasizing is that no tradition may be invested with a kind of diplomatic immunity to examination. No special privilege may be claimed for it.

When, on the other hand, we agitate for change, we need to be clear that it is not Scripture against which we are rebelling, but some unbiblical tradition which is therefore open to reform. If it is unbiblical in the sense of being clearly contrary to Scripture, then we should tackle it courageously and work hard for its abolition. If it is unbiblical in the sense of being not required by Scripture, then we must at least keep it under critical review.

More often than most of us know or care to admit, we invest our cultural ideas and practices with an authority, truth and timelessness which belong to Scripture alone. They form part of our security. When they are threatened, we feel threatened. So we play safe and vigorously defend them.

At other times we pay too little attention to the authority of Scripture and treat God's Word as if we can set it aside as easily as we can the opinions and traditions of men. Then we prove ourselves worldly Christians who have so thoroughly absorbed the secular world's antiauthority that we are not prepared even to live under the authority of God and of his Word by which he rules his people.

Contemporary Christians are called to walk this tightrope. We are neither to resist all change nor to agitate for total change. Further, even in matters which are open to change because Scripture gives this liberty, we are not to be mindless iconoclasts. Christians who believe in the God of history and in the activity of the Holy Spirit in past periods of church history can take no delight in change simply for change's sake. Some-

times, as Jesus said, "the old is better" (Luke 5:39) because it has stood the test of time. We must also be
sensitive to the conservatism of the older generation
of Christians; they cannot easily accustom themselves
to change, but can more easily be hurt and disturbed
by it. What we are called to is a wise discernment, in-
formed by a biblical perspective, so that we are appreciative of the legacy of the past and responsive to
the mood of the present. Only then can we apply to all
culture (in church and in society) a radical biblical
criticism and seek to change what under God we believe could be changed for the better.

The Church of England reformers of the sixteenth
century understood this principle well, at least in its
application to ecclesiastical reform. In the small print
at the beginning of the Book of Common Prayer
there is a foreword titled "*Of Ceremonies*, why some
be abolished and some retained." It was included in
the first reformed Prayer Book of 1549 and was
probably composed by Archbishop Cranmer himself.
He complains that

> in this our time the minds of men are so diverse
> that some think it is a great matter of conscience
> to depart from a piece of the least of their
> Ceremonies, they be so addicted to their old

customs; and again, on the other side, some be so new-fangled that they would innovate all things and so despise the old, that nothing can like [please] them but that is new.

Similarly, the preface, which explains the principles governing the revision of the Prayer Book in 1662, begins, "It hath been the wisdom of the Church of England, ever since the first compiling of her Publick Liturgy, to keep the mean between the two extremes, of too much stiffness in refusing, and of too much easiness in admitting, any variation from it." May God give us this same wisdom today, and may he also give us the courage to apply it not only to ecclesiastical affairs but in the social, ethical and political arenas as well.

Perhaps I can express myself in biological terms by saying that we need both Christian gadflies to sting and harry us into action for change and also Christian watchdogs who will bark loud and long if we show any signs of compromising biblical truth. Neither gadflies nor watchdogs are easy companions to live with. Nor do they find each other's company congenial. Yet the gadflies must not sting the watchdogs, nor must the watchdogs eat up the gadflies. They must learn to co-exist in God's church and to fulfill their respective roles by concentrating their attention on us, the generality of God's people, who badly need the ministry of both.

Having warned of the dangers of both too much change and too little, let me conclude this section by saying that the greater danger (at least among evangelicals) is to mistake culture for Scripture, to be too conservative and traditionalist, to be blind to those things in church and society which displease God and should therefore displease us, to dig our heels and our toes deep into the status quo and to resist firmly that most uncomfortable of all experiences, *change*.

4

Form & Freedom

I turn now from the polarization of the conservative and the radical to that of the structured and the unstructured. Secular structures are everywhere crumbling. There is a worldwide rebellion against rigid institutional forms and a universal feeling after freedom and flexibility. The Christian church, regarded in many parts of the world as one of the major Establishment structures, cannot escape this challenge of our times. Besides, the challenge comes from inside as well as outside. Many Christian young people are calling for a new and unstructured kind of Christianity shorn of the ecclesiastical encumbrances which have been inherited from the past.

Let me spell out the three main expressions of this mood. They concern the church and its ministry, the conduct of public worship and relations with fellow

Christians. It is seldom safe to generalize. Yet one may
say, first, that many are looking for churches without
a fixed form. Groups of Christians, now meeting in
many parts of the world, are breaking away from tradition and doing their own thing in their own way.
Second, there is a desire for worship services without
order, in which the minister no longer dominates
everything but congregational participation is encouraged, in which the organ is replaced by the guitar
and an ancient liturgy by the language of today, and in
which there is more freedom less form, more spontaneity less starch. Third, there is a rejection of denomi-
nationalism and a new emphasis on independency.
The younger generation is quite content to cut the
cords which tie them to the past and even to other
churches of the present. They want to call themselves
Christians without any denominational label.

Without question these three demands have con-
siderable cogency. They are strongly felt and forcefully
stated. We cannot simply write them off as the crazy
irresponsibilities of the young. There is a widespread
quest for the free, the flexible, the spontaneous, the
unstructured. The older and more traditional generation of Christians needs to understand it, to be sym-
pathetic to it and to go along with it as far as they can.
We all have to agree that the Holy Spirit can be—and

sometimes has been—imprisoned in our structures and stifled by our forms.

Nevertheless, there is something to be said on the other side. Freedom is not a synonym for anarchy. What case can be made, then, for forms and structures of some kind?

First, *a structured church*. Christians come from different church backgrounds and cherish different traditions. Yet most if not all of us will agree that the Founder of the church intended it to have a visible structure. True, the church has its invisible aspect, in that only "the Lord knows those who are his" (2 Timothy 2:19). Yet we cannot take refuge in the doctrine of the true church's invisibility in order to deny that Jesus Christ meant his people to be seen and known as such. He himself instituted baptism as the rite of initiation into his church, and baptism is a public and visible drama. He also instituted his Supper as the Christian fellowship meal by which the church identifies itself, excludes nonmembers and exercises discipline over members. Again, he appointed pastors to feed his flock. So, wherever you have baptism, the Lord's Supper and a pastorate, or, in traditional terms, a ministry and sacraments, you have a structure. It may be simpler and more flexible than in many historic denominations, but it remains a clear and defi-

nite structure. Moreover, one can strongly argue
the value of having a ministry and sacraments (or
ordinances) that are mutually acknowledged by different churches.

Second, *formal worship*. Speaking personally, I am
all for the spontaneous, exuberant, joyful, noisy
worship of the young, even if sometimes it can be
painful, as I once experienced in Beirut when my right
ear was only inches from the trombone! Some of our
services are far too formal, respectable and dull. At the
same time, in some modern meetings the almost total
loss of the dimension of reverence disturbs me. Some
believers seem to assume that the chief evidence of
the presence of the Holy Spirit is noise. Have we for-
gotten that a dove is as much an emblem of the Holy
Spirit as are wind and fire? When he visits his people
in power, he sometimes brings quietness, silence, reverence and awe. His still small voice is heard. People
bow down in wonder before the majesty of the living
God and worship: "The LORD is in his holy temple; let
all the earth be silent before him" (Habakkuk 2:20). I
am not suggesting that reverence and formality in-
variably go together, for informal gatherings can also
be reverent, while formal services can have dignity
and beauty without a true, spiritual reverence. But
where outward dignity and inward reverence are

found in conjunction, the worship that is offered is greatly honoring to God.

Third, *a connectional principle.* Most of us would want to insist on at least a degree of independence for the local church. Each local church, according to the New Testament, is a local, visible manifestation of the universal church. And the local church, not just the universal church, is called the temple of God and the body of Christ (the local church in 1 Corinthians 3:16; 12:27; and the universal church in Ephesians 2:19-22; 4:4, 16). Nevertheless, it is possible to carry this principle of the local church's autonomy too far and virtually to ignore all other Christians of the past and present. When this happens, the local church has become so self-contained as to despise the church of God in time and space.

We need therefore to remind ourselves of certain biblical truths which Christian people (especially the young) tend to forget. Are you interested only in the present? Are you the "now generation" who echoes with relish the famous dictum of Henry Ford that "history is bunk"? It sometimes seems so. Then what kind of God do you believe in? For the God of the Bible is the God of history, the God of Abraham, Isaac and Jacob, of Moses and the prophets, of Jesus Christ and his apostles and the postapostolic church, working out his purposes across the centuries. If God is the Lord of history, how can we ignore history or take no interest in it? He is also God of the whole church. The unity of the church derives from the unity of the Godhead. It is because there is one Father that there is only one family, because there is one Lord that there is only one faith, hope and baptism, and because there is one Spirit that there is only one body (see Ephesians 4:4-6).

So, if we cannot ignore the past, we cannot ignore the present either. True, the whole question of relations with other Christians is controversial and complicated, and certainly Scripture gives us no warrant to seek or secure unity without truth. But it gives us no warrant either to seek truth without unity. Independency is right. But so is fellowship in the common faith we profess.

Once again, my plea is that we do not polarize on this issue. There is a necessary place in Christ's church for both the structured and the unstructured, both the formal and the informal, both the dignified and the spontaneous, both independency and communion.

The early church sets us a healthy example in this matter. We read that, immediately after the day of Pentecost, the Spirit-filled believers "continued to meet together in the temple courts. They broke bread in their homes and ate together" (Acts 2:46). So they did not immediately reject the institutional church. They worked to reform it according to the gospel. And they supplemented the formal prayer services of the temple with their own home meetings. It seems to me that every local congregation should include in its program both the more dignified services in church and the more informal fellowship meetings in homes. The older, traditional church members who love the liturgy need to experience the freedom of home worship, while the younger church members who love noise and spontaneity need to experience the dignity and reverence of formal church services. The combination is very healthy.

5

EVANGELISM & SOCIAL ACTION

The fourth unnecessary polarization concerns our Christian evangelistic and social responsibilities.

It has always been a characteristic of evangelicals to occupy themselves with evangelism—so much so that one not infrequently comes across a confusion of terms as if *evangelical* and *evangelistic* mean the same thing. In our evangelical emphasis on evangelism we have understandably reacted against the so-called social gospel, which replaced individual salvation with social amelioration, and, despite the outstanding record of nineteenth-century evangelicals in social action, we have been suspicious of any such involvement ourselves. Or, if we have been socially active, we have tended to concentrate on good works of philanthropy (caring for the casualties of a sick society) and have steered clear of politics (concern for the underlying causes of a sick society).

Sometimes the polarization in the church has seemed complete, with some people exclusively pre-occupied with evangelism and others with socio-political action. As an example of the first, let us consider some groups of the so-called Jesus People. Now I am very far from wanting to be critical of the whole movement. Yet one of a number of hesitations I have concerns those Jesus communes which seem to have rejected society and withdrawn into their own fellowship, except for occasional evangelistic forays into the wicked world outside. Vernon Wishart, a minister of the United Church of Canada, wrote about the Jesus People in the November 1972 issue of his church's official magazine *Observer*. He described the movement as "a reaction to a deep cultural and social malaise" and an attempt to "overcome a flattening of the human spirit" caused by materialistic technocracy. He was appreciative of their genuine Christian commitment: "Like the early Christians they live simply, in a loving way, studying Scripture, breaking bread together and sharing resources." And he recognized that their intensely personal relation to Jesus and to one another was an antidote to the depersonalization of modern society. At the same time he saw this danger: "'Turning to Jesus can be a desperate attempt to turn away from the world in which he is incarnate. Like drugs, a Jesus religion can be an escape from our techno-culture." In these last sentences Vernon Wishart has put his finger on the main issue. If Jesus so loved the world that he entered it by incarnation, how can his followers claim to love it by seeking to escape from it? As Sir Frederick Catherwood has written, "To try to improve society is not worldliness but love. To wash your hands of society is not love but worldliness."[1]

The opposite polarization seems to have been evident at the assembly of the World Council of Churches' Commission on World Mission and Evangelism held in Bangkok in January 1973. Because it was titled "Salvation Today," many hoped that a fresh definition of salvation would emerge that was both faithful to Scripture and relevant to the modern world. But we were disappointed. The preparatory documents and the conference itself attempted to redefine salvation in almost entirely social, economic and political terms. It is true that there were references to personal salvation from sin, and that the purpose of the call for a ten-year moratorium on sending missionary money and personnel to Third World churches was to help them to become self-supporting. Nevertheless, the overall impression of Bangkok is that missionary and evangelistic labors are out of favor in ecumenical circles while the real mission of the church is to identify with the liberation movements of the day. "We see the struggles for economic justice, political freedom and cultural renewal as elements in the total liberation of the world through the mission of God."[2]

Of these two extremes the characteristic evangelical fault is the former, not the latter. We are not likely to mistake justice for salvation, but we have often talked and behaved as if we thought our only Christian responsibility toward non-Christian society was evangelism, the proclamation of the good news of salvation. There have, however, been welcome signs of change. We have become disillusioned with the "copout" mentality, the tendency to opt out of social responsibility, the traditional fundamentalist obsession with "microethics" (smoking, drinking and dancing) and the corresponding neglect of "macroethics" (race, violence, poverty, pollution, justice and freedom). There has also been among us a growing recognition of the biblical foundations, both theological and ethical, for Christian social action.

Theologically, there is a recovery of the doctrine of creation. We have tended to have a good doctrine of redemption and a bad doctrine of creation. Of course we have paid lip service to the truth that God is the Creator of all things, but we seem to have been blind to its implications. Our God has been too "religious," as if his main interests were worship services and prayer meetings attended by church members. Do not misunderstand me: God *does* take a delight in the prayers and praises of his people. But now we are beginning to see him also (as the Bible has always portrayed him) as the Creator, who is concerned for the secular world as well as the church, who loves all people and not Christians only, and who is interested in the whole of life and not merely in religion.

Ethically, there is a recovery of the duty of neighbor-love; that is, of the command to love our neighbor as we love ourselves. What this means in practice will be determined by who and what Scripture tells us our neighbor is. He or she is a person, a human being, created by God. And God created them neither bodyless souls (that we should love only their souls) nor soulless bodies (that we should be concerned exclusively for their physical welfare) nor even body-souls in isolation from society (that we should only care for them as individuals and not care about their society). No. God made humans spiritual, physical and social beings. As human beings our neighbors may be defined as "body-souls-in-community." Therefore the obligation to love our neighbors can never be reduced to the loving of only a bit of them. If we love our neighbors as God created them (which is God's command to us), then we shall inevitably be concerned for their total welfare, the welfare of their bodies, their souls and their society. Martin Luther King expressed this well: "Religion deals with both heaven and earth. . . . Any religion that professes to be concerned with the souls of men and is not concerned with the slums that doom them, the economic conditions that strangle them, and the social conditions that cripple them, is a dry-as-dust religion."[3] I think we should add that it is worse than that: It is actually a false religion.

It is true that the risen Lord Jesus left his church a Great Commission to preach, to evangelize and to make disciples. And this commission is still binding upon the church. But the commission does not supersede the commandment, as if "you shall love your neighbor" were now replaced by "you shall preach the gospel." Nor does it reinterpret neighbor-love in exclusively evangelistic terms. Instead, it enriches the commandment to love our neighbors by adding to it a new and Christian dimension, namely, the duty to make Christ known to them.

In urging that we should avoid the rather naive choice between evangelism and social action, I am not implying that every individual Christian must be equally involved in both. This would be impossible. Besides, we must recognize that God calls different people to different ministries and endows them with gifts appropriate to their calling. Certainly all Christians have the responsibility to love and serve their neighbors as the opportunity presents itself, but this will not inhibit them from concentrating—according to their vocation and gifts—on some particular concern, whether it be feeding the hungry, healing the sick, personal witness, home evangelism, local or national politics, community service, race relations, teaching or other good works of love.

Although every individual Christian must discover how God has called and gifted them, I venture to suggest that the local Christian church as a whole should be concerned for the local secular community as a whole. Once this is accepted in principle, individual Christians who share the same concerns would be encouraged to coalesce into study-and-action groups—not for action without prior study or for study without consequent action, but for both. Such responsible groups would give themselves to the prayerful consideration of a particular problem with a view to taking action in tackling it. One group might be concerned about evangelism in a new housing development in which (so far as is known) no Christians live or among a particular section of the local community—a residential hostel, a prison, students, school dropouts and so on. Another group might be burdened about immigrants and race relations, about a slum district and bad housing, about a retirement home or a hospital, about lonely retirees or single people in rented rooms, about a local abortion clinic or porn shop. The list of possibilities is almost endless. But if the members of a local congregation were to divide up the church's evangelistic and social responsibilities according to their concerns, callings and gifts, much constructive work could surely be done in the community.

I do not know any better statement of our double Christian responsibility, social and evangelistic, than that made during the Fourth Assembly of the World Council of Churches at Uppsala in 1968 by W. A. Visser 't Hooft, former WCC General Secretary:

> I believe that with regard to the great tension between the vertical interpretation of the Gospel as essentially concerned with God's saving action in the life of individuals and the horizontal interpretation of it as mainly concerned with human relationships in the world, we must get out of that rather primitive oscil-

lating movement of going from one extreme to the other. . . . A Christianity which has lost its vertical dimension has lost its salt and is not only insipid in itself but useless for the world. But a Christianity which would use the vertical preoccupation as a means to escape from its responsibility for and in the common life of man, is a denial of the Incarnation, of God's love for the world manifested in Christ. . . . It must become clear that church members who deny in fact their responsibility for the needy in any part of the world are just as much guilty of heresy as those who deny this or that article of the Faith.

My plea in this book has been for a balanced biblical Christianity, in which we avoid the common polarities of the Christian—and especially evangelical—world.

We need to emphasize both the intellectual and the emotional, remembering that nothing sets the heart on fire like truth; both the conservative and the radical, resolved to conserve Scripture but to evaluate culture according to Scripture; both the structured and the unstructured, for each can supplement the other; and both the evangelistic and the social, for neither can be a substitute, a cloak or an excuse for the other, since each stands on its own feet as an authentic expression of that love for our neighbor to which God the Lord still calls his people.

In at least these four areas (and they are not the only ones) we have good biblical warrant to replace a rather naive *either-or* with a mature *both-and*. Let us place our feet confidently and simultaneously on both poles. Don't let us polarize!

LIFE IN THE SPIRIT OF TRUTH

An Interview with John Stott

In 1995, Roy McCloughry interviewed John Stott for the British magazine *Third Way*. The interview was also republished by *Christianity Today* in the United States. The content of the interview further illuminates Stott's central themes of balanced Christianity and provides his perspectives on various issues facing evangelical Christianity.[1]

Your ministry now stretches back over fifty years. How have you changed over that time, both as a person and as a minister?

I'm afraid I was very naive when I was ordained. I was very much an activist more than a thinker. I saw needs and wanted immediately to meet them, and this crowded out my studies, really.

It was in the early days of my ministry that I learned the necessity of stepping back and seeing where I was going and having a monthly quiet day in which to be drawn up into the mind of God and look ahead for the next six or twelve months. That was an enormous benefit to me.

You've covered an enormous range of issues, theological, social, doctrinal and cultural. Has that been due to curiosity or to obligation as a minister?

A bit of both. Even before my conversion, I believe that God gave me a social conscience. When I was only fourteen years old, I started a society at school whose major purpose was to give baths to tramps. I had a great concern for these homeless, dirty men that I saw around the place. It was extremely naive.

We called it the ABC, because we thought they could understand that; but having decided on the letters we had to look around for words that would fit, and we came up with two: either "Always Be a Christian" or "The Association for the Benefit of the Community." It only lasted a few years and we never gave any baths to tramps; but we did some other good works, until the treasurer lent all the subscriptions to his brother, who spent everything.

My father was a doctor and a very high-minded, high-principled person, though not a Christian. He believed in a national health service before it was even dreamt about. My mother, too—we lived in Harley Street, and she was very concerned for the maids in the doctors' homes who had nothing to do on their afternoons off. She started the Domestic Fellowship. So, they both had a social conscience.

Some people might divide your ministry into two halves, one focused on pietism and one concerned with the very broadest social, cultural and economic aspirations of society. What caused this change?

Granted that it was something inherent in me from the beginning, I don't honestly think there was any individual or group. I think it was reading the Bible. As I read and studied and meditated, my vision of God grew and I came to see the obvious things: that he is not just interested in religion but in the whole of life and—in the old phrase—in justice as well as justification.

I don't see any dichotomy between the "pietistic" and the cultural and social. To me, they're two aspects of the same thing: a pursuit of the will of God. I have always been moved by the phrase "to hunger and thirst after righteousness"; but righteousness covers both personal holiness and social justice.

Some people might say that your commitment to the justice of God, expressed in social terms, had led to a watering-down of your commitment to the gospel.

I think that's rubbish, honestly. I don't think they can produce any evidence to substantiate that idea. I remain committed to evangelism. I have had the privilege of leading more than fifty university missions all over the world, and they spanned a period of twenty-five years, until I felt I was a little out of touch with the student generation, and too old.

I can honestly say that my social concerns have not in the very least diminished my zeal for evangelism. If anything, it's the other way round. What people could say is that I talk a lot about social action but don't do much about it. And that is true, because my calling is to be a pastor, and although I disagree with polarization between these two, I've often said I do believe in specialization.

Acts 6 is the obvious biblical basis for this: the apostles were not willing to be distracted from the ministry of the Word and prayer. In fact, the seven were appointed to handle the care of the widows. Both those works are called *diakonia*, "ministry"; both required Spirit-filled people to exercise them. Both were necessary, but one was social, the other was pastoral.

Don't some people fear that a renewed emphasis on social concern might muffle the call to evangelism?

There are a number of mission leaders, particularly Americans, who are frightened that we want missionaries, who are called more often than not to primary evangelism, to be distracted from that role in order to give themselves to sociopolitical work, which is none of their business.

I've really no wish for missionaries to change their role. I think there is a real need for evangelists who are not engaged in holistic mission because their calling is evangelism. I don't criticize Billy Graham because he simply preaches the gospel and doesn't engage in sociopolitical work—well, he does a bit, but not much—any more than we criticize the Good Samaritan for not preaching the gospel to the man who was assaulted by robbers.

It's partly the existential situation that determines what we concentrate on; it's partly our vocation. Everybody cannot do everything, as I keep saying to myself.

In all these debates and controversies, I have found

it increasingly important not only to listen to what people are saying but to try and listen to what lies behind what they're saying, and why it is that they feel so strongly.

How do you react to the emergence of the Reform group in the Church of England?

Although I have not felt able to join Reform, I am myself troubled by what troubles them, and committed to much of their program.

But I regret that Reform was launched without prior consultation with the Church of England Evangelical Council. I believe that CEEC could and should have embraced their concerns.

Secondly, the points of their program are disparate: some are essential to evangelical faith and witness, and should unite us; others are debatable and divide us.

Thirdly, I hope that Reform is not going back on the decision of Keele 1967 to work evangelically within the structures of the Church of England.

Do you still think the Anglican Church makes a good home for evangelicalism?

Yes, I think it's a good boat to fish from, but that's not the reason I'm a member of it.

There are three options, aren't there? The two extremes are to get out or cave in. The third is to stay in without giving in. The extremes are actually the easy options. Anybody can cave in: that's the way of the coward, the way of the feeble mind. To cave in is to stay in but to fail to hold on to your distinctive evangelicalism. You just compromise.

To get out is to say, "I can't bear this constant argument and controversy any longer." That also is an easy option. I know people have done it and suffered because they have given up a secure job and salary; but it's an easy option psychologically.

The difficult thing is to stay in and refuse to give in, because then you're all the time in tension with people with whom you don't altogether agree, and that is painful. I find it painful.

But no Christian can give unqualified allegiance to any institution. What, for you, would be the signals that it was time to leave the Church of England?

I've always felt that it's unwise to publish a list of these in advance. Nevertheless, I'm quite happy to talk about them. I think one's final decision to leave would be an exceedingly painful one, in a situation that I cannot envisage at the moment.

I would take refuge in the teaching of the New Testament, where the apostles seem to distinguish between major and minor errors. The major doctrinal errors concern the person and work of Christ. It's clear in 1 John that anyone who denies the divine-human person of Jesus is antichrist. So, if the church were officially to deny the incarnation, it would be an apostate church, and one would have to leave.

Then, there's the work of Christ. In Galatians, if anybody denies the gospel of justification by grace alone through faith alone, that is anathema: Paul calls down the judgment of God upon that person.

The major ethical issues—well, I suppose the best example is the incestuous offender in 1 Corinthians 5. Paul called on the church to excommunicate him. So, if you want me to stick my neck out, I think I would say that if the church were officially to approve of homosexual partnerships as a legitimate alternative to heterosexual marriage, this so far diverges from the sexual ethic of the Bible that I would find it exceedingly difficult to stay. I might want to stay on and fight for a few more years, but if they persisted I would have to leave.

It seems to me that evangelicalism has fragmented into different groups, with different heroes, different events, different publishers, different cultures. How should we think of ourselves now?

I don't mind plurality as long as it goes hand-in-hand with unity—but I suppose you could say I've given a great deal of my life to the preservation and development of the unity of the evangelical constituency, because it has been a great concern of mine.

I have never believed that our differences have been great enough to warrant a fragmentation. I don't mind people founding their own societies and going after their own thing—again, it's an example of specialization—provided they still recognize that we belong to one another.

I do have to add that I'm worried about a redevelopment of the kind of liberal evangelicalism which flourished before the Second World War but which really had no message, no cutting edge. I don't want to see us going back to that. It had a loose doctrine of the Bible: they talked about its authority, but in practice the Bible was not their authority.

What are the current causes of our fragmentation?

Well, we fragment over what we regard as issues of principle—but often the real reason is personal, isn't it? When we're afraid, we withdraw into our own fellowships and ghettos where we feel secure with like-minded people. I'm aware of that fear in myself; it's part of our basic human insecurity. We're looking for contexts in which we can be supported rather than questioned.

I'm afraid that in some cases it's worse than that—

it's a simple question of ambition. There is a great deal of empire-building among us. The only empire in which we should be interested is the kingdom of God, but I fear some people are building their own.

Of the issues of principle, what concerns you most?

The uniqueness and finality of Jesus Christ in an increasingly pluralistic world is one. The debate about whether we go for exclusivism, inclusivism or pluralism. Then there's the homosexual question, and the whole question of sexual ethics.

How is it that some people feel able to say, "We are part of the Anglican tradition, which has Scripture at its heart, and yet we can accept these things"?

They base their position on the cultural element in Scripture. What they're trying to say is that Paul had very little knowledge of psychosexuality and we can't possibly be bound by him. They seem to have no qualms about rejecting apostolic teaching.

So, the church must recover its prophetic voice and reject both the idea that ethics evolve and the notion that love obliges us to capitulate to the modernist view of things. Is that prophetic voice too dull in the Anglican Church at the moment?

Oh yes. Too dull and too mute. We need a voice that is

essentially positive, not just negative—for example, on the family, or the joy of sexual intercourse and so on.

I don't know why we are always caught on the defensive and are retroactive instead of proactive. I don't think it is something in our makeup as evangelicals. I sometimes wonder if it is that God has not given us many leaders who are visionaries.

The evangelical renaissance of the last fifty years has really been one of biblical scholarship. What we have lacked is systematic or creative theologians. I believe we have one in Alister McGrath; I am sure we had one in Jim Packer, before he left the country. But we have very few theologians who are really far-sighted and give us a vision that will unite and inspire and enthuse us.

Why is that?

I just don't know. I wish I did. It grieves me. We certainly need to pray for such to be raised up.

Is it something to do with our perception of truth in terms of orthodoxy, which makes it difficult to be creative because that involves taking risks?

Yes, there is something in that. Evangelicalism is fundamentally loyal to a past revelation, and because we are tied forever to what God did and said in the historic Jesus, we look back more often than we look forward.

In my debate with David Edwards (published in

1989 as *Evangelical Essentials*[2]), I drew a distinction between the liberal, the fundamentalist and the evangelical. The liberal, to me, is like a gas-filled balloon which takes off into the ether and is not tethered to the earth in any way; the fundamentalist is like a caged bird, unable to escape at all. To me, the true evangelical is like a kite, which flies high but at the same time is always tethered.

I long to see that developed, I must say; but it does need a particularly unusual combination of loyalty to the past and creativity for the future.

You yourself have fallen foul of some evangelicals. I hear that some of your reflections on the nature of eternal punishment were considered uncongenial to orthodoxy by some people, particularly in the States.

Well, that's a polite way of putting it.

In *Evangelical Essentials*, I described as "tentative" my suggestion that "eternal punishment" may mean the ultimate annihilation of the wicked rather than their eternal conscious torment. I would prefer to call myself agnostic, as are a number of New Testament scholars I know. In my view, the biblical teaching is not plain enough to warrant dogmatism. There are awkward texts on both sides of the debate.

The reaction to what I said about this was mixed. Some evangelicals responded thoughtfully and theologically, others with inflexible dogmatism—I find myself increasingly out of sympathy with excessive evangelical dogmatism—and a third group, especially in the US, was positively hysterical in its denunciation. Many people went into print without even having bothered to read what I had written.

It's a very distressing thing about evangelicalism—we are not good at responsible domestic debate. But the hallmark of an authentic evangelical is not the uncritical repetition of old traditions but the willingness to submit every tradition, however ancient, to fresh biblical scrutiny, and, if necessary, reform.

Did that experience suggest that the British evangelical tradition is diverging from the US tradition? Do you see differences between the two cultures?

I've learnt long ago that one cannot generalize about anything American, even the evangelical scene. Somebody has worked out that there are about twenty different American evangelicalisms. But if I may generalize, I think there is a greater willingness to trust one another as evangelicals in this country. Fellowship in America often seems to be based more on suspicion than on trust. I don't know why that is.

How would you advise theologians to try to think creatively in the light of orthodoxy?

All I can say is that I don't think any of us is wise to express ourselves in a creative or questioning manner without first testing out what we want to say within the Christian community. I think it is part of our loyalty to that community that we allow it to criticize or comment on what we may want to say.

In your debate with David Edwards, you both seemed to reach a genuine understanding of and respect for each other's position. Do you feel that evangelicals have got things to learn from the liberal tradition?

I wonder what to say. David Edwards, I think, as a self-styled liberal is crying out for a certain intellectual and academic freedom which can move with the times and respond to what he continually calls "the climate of educated opinion today," without being tethered to anything more than the love of God manifested in Jesus of Nazareth. I don't think that's an unfair summary. But all the time he's pulling at the tether, and that's the great difference between us.

He would say that we evangelicals have a poor doctrine of the Holy Spirit, because we don't think the Spirit is continuing to teach and to "lead us into all the truth." Now, I believe that that text, John 16:13, is the most misunderstood and manipulated text in the whole of the Bible, because every branch of Christendom claims it.

It's a key text for the Roman Catholic Church. "He will lead you into all the truth." Who? The successors of the apostles. The liberal quotes it. The charismatic quotes it: "He'll lead me." But even the most elementary hermeneutical principle will tell us that the "you" means the apostles. Jesus said, "I have much more to say to you, but you cannot bear it now." Who is he addressing? The apostles. "But when the Spirit comes, he will do what I have not been able to do; he will lead you into the truth which I wanted to give you but you weren't able to take it." It must be the apostles. We cannot change the identity of the "you" in the middle of the sentence.

So, the fulfillment of that prophecy is in the New Testament. The major ministry of the Holy Spirit has been to lead the apostles into all the truth and to give us in the New Testament this wonderful body of truth that remains our authority. Now, that does not mean that the ministry of the Holy Spirit has ceased. It means that it has changed from the revelation of new truth to a profounder perception and application of old truth. If you like, he has moved from revelation to illumination.

Although I may be slightly overstating it, I want to say that God has no more to teach us than he has taught us in Christ. It is inconceivable that there should be a higher revelation than God has given in his incarnate Son. But although God has no more to teach us, we have a great deal more to learn. And although he has no more to give us than he has given us in Christ, we have a great deal more to receive.

Some people feel that evangelicals adapt, eventually, to changing circumstances, whereas Catholicism stands firm like a rock. Those who say there is a loss of authority in our world are tending toward Rome—

Or Orthodoxy.

Indeed. Do you think there is something about Rome which is rightly attractive?

Yes. The true evangelical wants both liberty and authority. We want to ask questions, to think, to pry, to peer, to probe, to ponder. We want to do all these things, but within a framework of submission to an ultimate authority. But we're asking questions about our authority: what does it mean and how does it apply? So, we experience an uneasy tension between liberty and authority.

I couldn't myself find a lodging place either in Catholicism or in liberalism, because one seems to me to major on authority with little room for liberty, while the other emphasizes liberty with very little room indeed for authority.

An anthology of your writings, *Authentic Christianity*,[3] includes this quotation: "The word 'Christian' occurs only three times in the Bible. Because of its common misuse we could profitably dispense with it." Since the word "evangelical" doesn't appear at all and is also misused, should we dispense with it, too?

We could in theory, for the same reason. The words that are used in the New Testament most frequently are "believer," "brother" or "sister," "child of God." There isn't a word that the Bible itself gives us to which we have to be loyal.

But the reason I want to stick to "evangelical" is a historical one. It has expressed a recognizable tradition, to which I still feel I belong (and am proud and thankful to belong), and I want to take my stand not only on Scripture but in that tradition.

Does it alarm you to hear people calling themselves "postevangelical"?

Yes. I don't know what they mean, but it does alarm me.

If you are "post" anything, you are leaving something behind, and I want to know what it is. If it's our many faults and failures, fine—but that's not post-evangelicalism, it's post-twisted-evangelicalism.

What are the weaknesses of evangelicalism?

We've discussed our rugged individualism and the difficulty we have in cooperating with one another. Another, I think, is our dogmatism. Instead of remembering Deuteronomy 29:29, we are dogmatic about even the things which God has kept secret. We're often not prepared to admit a certain agnosticism, which is a very evangelical thing, if we are alluding to what God has not revealed.

We have many weaknesses. I'm sure there are plenty more if I were to go on.

Again in *Authentic Christianity*, you say: "Evangelism is the major instrument of social change. For the gospel changes people, and changed people can change society." Isn't that really a ruggedly individualistic picture of social change? It certainly surprised me.

I wonder what the context of that was. I think it's from *Issues Facing Christians Today*, where I list four or five instruments for social change. I put evangelism first because Christian social responsibility depends on socially responsible Christians, and they are the fruit of evangelism.

Having said that, I would also want to make the complementary point that Christians are not the only people who have benefited or reformed society. We evangelicals do have a very naive view. Take marriage: people say, "They have got to be converted and then they'll have a good marriage." But there are Christians who don't have good marriages, and there are plenty of excellent marriages among people who are not Christians. Morality and social conscience are not limited to Christian people.

Do you think that our emphasis on "the Christian mind" may have prevented us from fully affirming the wisdom to be found outside the church?

What you mean is: should we pay attention to the wisdom literature of other religions?

And of people with no religion.

Yes, we certainly should, even if it is with reservations and a desire to bring their thinking to the ultimate touchstone of biblical authority.

I suppose the key text would be John 1:9, which says that the *logos*, the Son of God before the incarnation, is the true light, coming into the world and giving light to everybody. I believe that is the right translation, that he is constantly coming into the world—indeed, he has never left it, because the world was made by him and so he is in the world. He was in the world even before he came into it in the incarnation, and as the *logos* he is giving light to everybody.

So, there is a certain light of common sense, of reason, of conscience, that everybody has. And because also they're made in the image of God, although, to be sure, reason is fallen and fallible, nevertheless it still operates.

For those two reasons, the divine *logos* and the human *logos*, if you like, we should listen respectfully to what other people are saying, even if at the end of the day we have the liberty to say, "No, that is wrong, because the Bible teaches otherwise."

Why is the church so often the last to join a protest movement? It may in time take the lead and it may speak with the greatest integrity, against jingoism or apartheid or nuclear weapons or the abuse of the environment or whatever; but these movements are often started by others.

Well, that has not always been true—the slave trade is a good example, isn't it, and, I suppose, Shaftesbury's reforms in relation to mental illness and so on.

Nevertheless, by and large what you say is true. Why? First, because we're busy—we're busy evangelizing and doing other things, mostly in the church.

We don't always demand our liberty from the church in order to be active in the world.

Our attention is elsewhere?

Yes. Elsewhere is more congenial to us than being anywhere in the world.

Second, we have such a strong doctrine of fellowship and are so clear about our responsibility not to be unequally yoked with unbelievers that we have seldom learnt Francis Schaeffer's well-known term that we can be "co-belligerents" even if we are not in active spiritual fellowship with one another.

That's all very well, but some people might say that the church is simply very conservative. It only joins these movements for change under pressure from secular forces in society.

I wish it were always Christians who took the initiative in seeking needed social change—but I am still thankful when others take the initiative and Christians follow, even under secular pressure.

We must not set secular fashion and the Holy Spirit over against each other, as being always and inevitably incompatible. Public opinion isn't always wrong. What is wrong is to bow down before it uncritically, like reeds shaken by the wind. Why should the Holy Spirit not sometimes use public opinion to bring his people into line? He seems to have done so on a number of occasions in the debate between science and faith.

Is it possible that evangelicals may never learn that evangelism and social action are not alternatives?

I hope not. I believe we have changed, and we can change more. We need to go on bearing witness to truth as we have been given to see it, in our interior, domestic dialogue.

Do you think we have yet got the balance between evangelism and social action right?

I think there are notable examples of groups and individuals who are seeking to recover their mislaid social conscience, but no, we've got a long way further to go. What we need more than anything else is more models of integrated mission, so that people can see that it works without neglecting anything to which we have been called.

What is the theological basis for Christian involvement today? Is it enough to speak of "salt and light"?

First, there is the nature of God himself. God is interested in and concerned about more than religion: he is the God of creation as well as of the covenant. He is the lover of justice: this is his nature. He is the kind of

God who protects and champions the oppressed. And if that is the kind of God he is, then clearly his people have got to be the same.

Second, there is the doctrine of human beings. If you concentrate exclusively on the eternal salvation of the soul, you give the impression that a human being is simply a soul floating in the ether. When I was a student, we were brought up on the phrase "a love for souls." I remember reading a book called *A Passion for Souls*. But I have never had a passion for souls. I can't envisage a soul as being an appropriate object of love or affection.

Human beings are more than souls; they are "body-souls-in-a-community." If I truly love my neighbor, the second great commandment obliges me to love and serve him or her in their physical, social and spiritual dimension.

I could go on—there is so much. Almost every biblical doctrine has some relation to this whole question.

Nevertheless, when you see young people who have a passion for evangelism, they are motivated by that idea of a lost soul, even if it is incorrect. Is there an equivalent spur for people involved in social action? If someone said to you, "My calling is social action. Give me the same passion!", what would you say?

I think I would talk of the doctrine of man, male and female, made in the image of God—the unique dignity and worth of human beings. I would quote William Temple, who said, "My worth is what I am worth to God, and that is a marvelous great deal, because Christ died for me." And I would say that the ministry of Jesus in life and death exhibits the enormous value of human beings.

Then, I would want to back up that biblical theme with examples from throughout history. Take Mother Teresa, for example, who sees this woman on the pavement of Calcutta, with awful sores infested with live maggots, and she kisses her and picks her up. She sees an intrinsic value in her.

That, surely, is what has motivated people. That is why the word *humanization*, which was first adopted in the World Council of Churches, is something we evangelicals ought to have taken up. Anything that dehumanizes human beings should be an outrage to us, because God has made them in his image. The whole concept of the dehumanization of human beings, and the deliverance of human beings from anything that dehumanizes, ought to inspire people, and has inspired people.

Authentic Christianity **records you saying in 1981: "What will posterity see as the chief Christian**

blind spot of the last quarter of the 20th century? I do not know. But I suspect it will have something to do with the economic oppression of the Third World and the readiness with which Western Christians tolerate it, and even acquiesce to it."

I did, I think, mention three blind spots. The nuclear horror was another one: evangelicals were the last people to make a statement about the immorality of weapons of indiscriminate destruction. I think the third one was the environment.

There is a great deal in the Bible about God's concern for the poor. Poverty—not poverty in the sense of simplicity, but in the sense of lacking the basic wherewithal for survival—is not really on our evangelical conscience yet. Partly because many people have not traveled and seen oppressive poverty with their own eyes—although, to be sure, they have seen the pictures on television.

Are we too ready in the West to accept the view that a successful church is also an affluent one?

I suppose it is because some people see prosperity as a mark of God's blessing, even today, that they can't come to terms with poverty. I think we have to have the courage to reject the health-and-wealth gospel absolutely. It's a false gospel.

I was very thankful that Benny Hinn publicly repented of teaching it.

Do you think the idea that God wants us to be comfortable because he loves us presents a threat to a cutting-edge spirituality?

Well, we're sitting in a very comfortable flat as we talk, and it's easy to say! But I do think that comfort is dangerous, and we should constantly be reexamining our lifestyle.

The New Testament is beautifully balanced on this. Paul avoids both extremes, not least in 1 Timothy 4 and 6. Asceticism is a rejection of the good gifts of the good Creator. Its opposite is materialism—not just possessing material things but becoming preoccupied with them. In between asceticism and materialism is simplicity, contentment and generosity, and those three things should mark all of us.

It's not a question of rules and regulations about our income and how many rooms we have and how many cars. It's a question of these principles of simplicity, contentment and generosity, over against covetousness, materialism and asceticism, that we have to apply to our living all the time. We need to give away what we are not using, because if we don't use it, we don't need it.

You've seen a great deal of poverty around the world. Do you perceive a difference between the Christianity of the poor and the Christianity of the rich?

Yes, I do. In the Old Testament, there is a fundamental association between material and spiritual poverty. Often, you are not sure what is meant by "the poor." But they tend to be those who are materially poor and who on account of that poverty need to put their trust in God with a greater strength than if they were rich and so self-dependent.

My own understanding is that in the Sermon on the Mount—which may have been a concentrated period of instruction—Jesus said both "Blessed are you poor" (as he is quoted in Luke) and "Blessed are the poor in spirit" (as in Matthew). I think there is a blessedness attaching to both. The kingdom of God is a blessing to the materially poor because it affirms their dignity and relieves their poverty; it is also a blessing, a free gift, to the spiritually poor. So, there is a sense in which poverty is an aid to faith and riches are a barrier to faith.

I want to add that all these terms—*simplicity, contentment, generosity, wealth*—are comparative. There is no absolute simplicity or poverty. I go into my little kitchen and I have not only running water but constant hot water. That would be regarded as the height of luxury in some parts of the world, yet we don't regard it as that, and comparatively speaking in this country it isn't.

We need to feel the challenge of Jesus to us in the light of our own situation and circumstances.

Is God's kingdom a blessing to the poor even if they do not recognize that they are poor in spirit?

No, I think the two blessings go together.

Do the poor tend to see themselves as poor in spirit?

Some do. Their material poverty helps them to see their need of Christ. Others, however, become bitter and can't listen to the gospel. What is the African phrase? "An empty belly has no ears." When they're as poor as that, they can't respond to the gospel. It's rather like the Israelites when Moses came and told them about the exodus: "They did not listen to him because of their cruel bondage."

Presumably, then, we need to listen carefully to the liberation theologians.

Yes!

They say that the Scriptures were written against a background of poverty and are most truly understood when they are read with the eyes of the poor.

I'm very keen on crosscultural Bible study groups, so that we can help each other to listen to the word of God, but I don't think it is true to say that the poor necessarily have a greater insight. We all come to Scripture with our presuppositions and our cultural defenses, and these may be very different from one another's. The liberation theologian and the Marxist also have their cultural defenses.

What we need to do in intercultural Bible study groups is to cry to God to use us to one another in breaking through those defenses.

Can we turn to the charismatic movement? How have your views changed since *Baptism and Fullness*[4]?

Baptism and Fullness was the second edition—the first was *The Baptism and Fullness of the Holy Spirit*.[5] I practically rewrote the book, principally because I felt I had been less than generous in my evaluation of the movement. So, I wanted to put on record that I had no doubt that God had blessed the charismatic movement to both individuals and local churches. It would be quite impossible and improper to deny that.

Maybe I should go on positively a little bit. I do believe in the Holy Spirit! I believe the Christian life is inconceivable without the Holy Spirit. The Christian faith and life depend entirely upon the Holy Spirit: he convicts us of sin, he opens our eyes to see the truth as it is in Jesus, he causes the new birth to take place, he bears witness with our spirit that we are the children of God, he transforms us into the image of Christ, he is the earnest of our final inheritance, and so on. Every stage and every part of the Christian life is impossible without the Holy Spirit.

So, I believe in him; but I still believe that some of the distinctive doctrines of charismatic Christians are not as honoring to him as they think they are, and are in fact mistaken.

What I find difficult is the stereotyping of Christian experience—that everybody has to go through the same two hoops. I don't see that in the New Testament. I see the emphasis on the new birth—and the New Testament bends over backwards in its attempt to find adequate phraseology to define the new birth. It speaks not only of rebirth but of re-creation and resurrection, and nothing could be greater than that. It seems to me we are bound to go askew if we put any subsequent experience on a level higher than the original one.

As for the gifts, I simply think that many charismatics focus on the wrong ones. There are at least twenty identified in the New Testament, and these lists are so random that there are probably many more that are not included. But the Pentecostal still concentrates on the three supernatural gifts of healing, prophecy and tongues.

Actually, I think the most important gift today, measured by Paul's principle that we should excel in those that build up the church, is teaching. Nothing builds up the church like the truth, and we desperately need more Christian teachers all over the world. I often say to my charismatic friends, "If only you would concentrate on praying that God would give teachers to his church, who could lead all these new converts into maturity in Christ, it would be more profitable."

Could the development of the movement bring about an existential form of Christianity? Just as liberals read Scripture in the light of its relevance to culture, could the charismatics read it in the light of its relevance to experience?

I think that's well put, and I want to endorse it. I wish I'd thought of it first!

Mind you, I don't want to denigrate experience. I don't want charismatics to say of me, as they often do, "He's a dry old stick." Because I'm not, actually. I'm a much more emotional person than people realize. I thank God that he hasn't made me a fish, cold and slippery. I'm very thankful to be a human being, with all the emotional passion and fervor, as well as intellectual concern, which that entails.

I do believe in emotion, I do believe in experience. The Christianity of the New Testament is undoubtedly an experiential faith, in which deep feelings are involved. But I want to combine clear thinking with deep feeling.

I find that mind and emotion are kept together very much in the New Testament. I have always loved, for example, the Emmaus walk: "Did not our hearts burn within us when he opened to us the scriptures?" It was through their mind that their heart began to burn. We have to recognize the important place of experience— but our experience does have all the time to be checked against biblical teaching. Otherwise, it will become an ungodly and un-Christian existentialism.

Have you yourself had experiences of God which could be called "charismatic"?

I want to say yes to the first part of the sentence and no to the second. Certainly, God has given me in his goodness some profound spiritual experiences, both when I've been alone and even more in public worship, when tears have come to my eyes, when I've perceived something of his glory.

I can remember one particular occasion, when we were singing "At the name of Jesus every knee shall bow," I did really break down, because I saw again the supreme exaltation of Jesus to the right hand of the Father. I have had other profound experiences which have moved me to the core of my being. But I wouldn't say that any of them has been a traditional charismatic experience such as speaking in tongues. And they have not been disassociated from the mind. In 1 Corinthians 14, Paul is all the time saying, "You mustn't let these experiences bypass your mind." The mind is involved, though the experience goes beyond it.

But I know what Paul meant in Romans 5 about the love of God being shed abroad in our hearts. I also know what he meant in Romans 8 about the Spirit bearing witness with our spirit that we are the children of God.

Do you think the charismatic movement will finally prove to have strengthened or distracted the church?

I'm not a prophet; I can't look forward. I think it's bound to have been more blessing than the opposite. But I'm very worried about the anti-intellectual aspect of it. Not all charismatics are anti-intellectual, I know, but there are very many who are. They dismiss me, again, because they say I'm not open to the supernatural on account of my Western rationalism. I disagree with that. I'm not a rationalist and I'm absolutely open to God; but I refuse to surrender my mind.

That's why I think Jim Packer's book *Keep in Step with the Spirit* is so important. It's a most unusual, maybe unique, combination of the open and the critical. On the one hand, he stands in the Puritan tradition and so takes very seriously the prohibition "Do not quench the Spirit!" He is determined to give the Holy Spirit his freedom. On the other hand, he subjects the claims and performance of the charismatic movement to a rigorous biblical critique.

This is an unusual combination because those of us who are open are usually uncritical, while those of us who are critical are usually closed.

But evangelicals, too, have been accused of anti-intellectualism in two books: Mark Noll's *The Scandal of the Evangelical Mind* and Os Guinness's *Fit Bodies, Fat Minds*. This trend seems to be more pervasive than just an existential, experiential thing.

I agree. It has been characteristic of much evangelicalism (but even more of Pentecostalism). There are notable exceptions, and thank God for them.

I think we need to encourage each other in the proper use of the mind. Preachers are still the key people; the church is always a reflection of the preaching it receives, and I don't think it is an exaggeration to say that the low standards of Christian living throughout the world are due more than anything else to the low standards of Christian preaching and teaching.

If we can recover true expository preaching as being not only exegesis but an exposition and application of the word of God, then the congregations will learn it from us and go and do the same thing themselves. We need to help our congregations to grasp and use the hermeneutical principles that we ourselves are using. We need to be so careful in the development of our evangelical hermeneutic that the congregation says, "Yes, I see it. That is what the text means and it couldn't mean anything else."

The worst kind of preaching there is allows people to say, "Well, I'm sorry, I don't agree with you. I think you're twisting the Scripture."

You seem to me to have changed your position on gender. Certainly, your later writings present a different view of the status and role of women. What has brought this about?

What has helped me most in struggling with this issue is a growing understanding of the need for "cultural transposition." This is based on the recognition that although biblical truth is eternal and normative in its substance, it is often expressed in changeable cultural terms.

The Lausanne Covenant described Scripture as "without error in all that it affirms." Our duty is to determine what it does affirm—that is, what God is teaching, promising or commanding in any given passage. When we have identified this, we have the further task of reclothing this unchanging revelation in appropriate modern cultural dress. The purpose is not to dodge awkward teachings of Scripture, still less to foster disobedience, but to make our obedience contemporary.

If we apply this principle to the role of women, it seems clear to me that masculine "headship" (which I believe refers to responsibility rather than authority) is a permanent and universal truth, because Paul roots it in creation. And what creation has established, no culture is able to destroy. We have no liberty to disagree with the apostle Paul.

But we still need to ask, "What are the appropriate cultural expressions of that in the church today?" For one thing, we may drop the wearing of veils. Is it possible, then, that the requirement of silence is similarly a first-century cultural application which is not necessarily applicable today?

This, if I remember rightly, was the position we adopted at the National Evangelical Anglican Congress in 1977. We expressed the view that a woman could be ordained, and so could teach men, but that an appropriate contemporary expression of masculine headship would be for her to belong to a local pastoral team, of which a man would be the head.

I still hold this view, although, of course, I know it has been overtaken by history.

You have said that Christians are optimists but not utopians. Are you optimistic about the church? Do you feel that the next generation of leaders are adequately equipped?

Yes, I think I must reply in the affirmative. Elderly people of my generation always have difficulty in recognizing the gifts of the young, or younger, but surely, as I look around, there are men and women of most remarkable gifts that God is raising up.

Yet we are not utopians. We cannot build the kingdom of God on earth. We are waiting for the new heaven and the new earth, which will be the home of righteousness and peace. But meanwhile I'm an optimist, because I don't think pessimism and faith are easy bedfellows. I believe that God is at work in the world, I believe that the gospel is the power of God unto salvation to every believer, and I believe that the church can be salt and light in the community. Both salt and light are influential commodities: they change the environment in which they are placed.

Is it easier now to find outstanding Christian leadership in the Third World than in our own society?

It's very difficult to compare the two, because they are very different. God is certainly giving leadership in Third World churches which compares beautifully with the kind of leadership there was in the developing world decades ago, when missions were still suppressing the churches. But now that national churches have taken over responsibility from the missions, and are developing their own identity and their own leadership, it's wonderful to see the caliber of leadership that God is giving.

What advice would you give to the new generation of the church's leaders?

I'd want to say so many things. But my main exhortation would be this: Don't neglect your critical faculties. Remember that God is a rational God, who has made us in his own image. He invites and expects us to explore his double revelation, in nature and Scripture, with the minds he has given us, and to go on in the development of a Christian mind to apply his marvelous revealed truth to every aspect of the modern and the postmodern world.

NOTES

Chapter One: Unity, Liberty & Charity

[1]William Carus, ed., *Memoirs of the Life of the Rev. Charles Simeon*, (New York: Rober Carter, 1847), p. 600.

Chapter Two: Intellect & Emotion

[1]Quoted by R. W. Burtner and R. E. Chiles in *A Compend of Wesley's Theology* (Nashville: Abingdon Press, 1954), p. 26.

[2]Alvin Toffler, *Future Shock* (New York: Bantam, 1971), p. 331.

[3]Pamela Hansford Johnson, *On Iniquity* (New York: Scribner, 1967), pp. 18 and 24.

[4]Quoted by Ralph G. Turnbull in *A Minister's Obstacles* (Westwood, NJ: Fleming H. Revell, 1946), p. 97.

[5]D. Martyn Lloyd-Jones, *Preaching and Preachers* (Grand Rapids: Eerdmans, 1971), p. 97.

Chapter Three: Conservative & Radical

[1]Colin Buchanan, E. L. Mascall, J. I. Packer and Willesden, *Growing into Union* (London: SPCK, 1970), p. 103.

[2]Toffler, *Future Shock*, p. 19.

Chapter Five: Evangelism & Social Action

[1]Sir Frederick Catherwood, "Reform or Revolution?" in *Is Revolution Change?* ed. Brian Griffiths (Downers Grove, IL: InterVarsity Press, 1972), p. 35.

[2]*Bangkok Assembly* (New York: World Council of Churches, 1973), p. 89.

[3]Coretta King, *My Life with Martin Luther King, Jr.* (New York: Avon Books, 1970), p. 127.

Chapter Six: Life in the Spirit of Truth—An Interview with John Stott

[1]The interview is reproduced here with the permission of the original interviewer and publications. Available online at www.thirdwaymagazine.co.uk/editions/no-edition/high-profile/life-in-the-spirit-of-truth.aspx and in abridged form at www.christianitytoday.com/ct/2003/septemberweb-only/9-1-51.0.html.

[2]David L. Edwards and John Stott, *Evangelical Essentials* (Downers Grove, IL: InterVarsity Press, 1989).

[3]John Stott, *Authentic Christianity*, ed. Timothy Dudley-Smith (Downers Grove, IL: InterVarsity Press, 1995).

[4]Stott, *Baptism and Fullness* (Downers Grove, IL: InterVarsity Press, 1975).

[5]Stott, *The Baptism and Fullness of the Holy Spirit* (Downers Grove, IL: InterVarsity Press, 1964).